king's singers

# English Renaissance

The Colour of Song
Volume 1



ISBN 0-634-01563-X

k's
*the colour of song*

Exclusively Distributed By
HAL•LEONARD® CORPORATION
7777 W. Bluemound Rd. P.O. Box 13819 Milwaukee, WI 53213

# ENGLISH RENAISSANCE
## The Colour of Song (Vol. 1)

At a performance by the King'singers, audiences throughout the world experience a wide range of emotions depicted in the group's vast repertoire – joy, sadness, love, anger, jealousy, laughter. The range of vocal colours used is no less wide, and by the end of the concert the audiences perhaps realize that the human voice is capable of much more than simply speaking or singing. The King'singers call this total experience "The Colour of Song." This series of songbooks aims to reflect the variety of repertoire and performing technique which is found in each of the musical periods the King'singers explore in their concert work – from Byrd to the Beatles! We hope these collections will enrich your concert repertoire.

The English Renaissance period produced composers who were held in great respect across the whole of Europe. This, coupled with the rise in unaccompanied choral music as a form, both sacred and secular, makes this particular period very productive when a group like the King'singers is searching for repertoire, but at the same time makes it difficult when having to select the pieces to include in this volume. We hope our choices will interest you and possibly inspire you to search for additional pieces yourselves.

## Arrangement/Performance Notes

**All Creatures Now Are Merry Minded** *(John Bennett, c1575?-1614?)*
This and the following piece are both contained in Thomas Morley's famous *The Triumphs of Oriana* collection of 1601 in honour of Queen Elizabeth I. This piece can rush if started too fast on the opening long notes. Phrases like "Birds over her do hover" need graceful handling. Like many of these pieces, it shouldn't be dominated by the top line, which is not really a "tune" as such. All voices are important in order to get across the harmonic and rhythmic interest which the composer has incorporated.

**As Vesta Was from Latmos Hill Descending** *(Thomas Weelkes, 1576?-1623?)*
Of all the madrigals in *The Triumphs of Oriana*, this has to be the finest (and we recently recorded all 24 of them, so we should know!). Musical word painting is abundant and exquisitely done: from simple touches like "ascending," "descending," "running down amain" and the use of the appropriate number of voices in the "First two by two,... all alone" section, to the more subtle augmentation of the "Long live fair Oriana" motive in the bass part, with the most augmented word being, of course, "Long." With all this comes a need for a wide range of vocal colour: try an excited, slightly off-the-voice sound for "came running down amain," a forlorn tone for "all alone" (this could benefit from being a solo voice) and a real brassy quality for the chorus "Then sang the shepherds..." Rumour has it that the collection was put together

in a hurry to cheer up the Queen. If that is the case, Weelkes shows no signs that having to rush his composing worried him, and if our former Sovereign knew anything at all about music, she would have had a smile as broad as her father when she heard this one!

**Drop, Drop, Slow Tears** *(Orlando Gibbons, 1583-1625)*
This hymn should be sung very simply, with careful attention paid to expressing the beautiful poetry. Use clear consonants and clear vowel sounds.

**Fire, Fire** *(Thomas Morley, c1557-1602)*
Thomas Morley's madrigal is a plea to extinquish the flames of a fire – not in the poet's house, but a fire of passion burning within his heart. It is a piece that should not be taken seriously as far as the text is concerned. We joke with audiences when we sing this that the "Fa la la" refrain is used in place of what the poet really wanted to say, which of course is too explicit – a form of Elizabethan censorship if you like! It should be fast, but only if the rhythm is strict and can be maintained with a lot of energy. Avoid the temptation to rush or to lose intensity at any point. There aren't many words, but those there are should be very clear and crisp. In a word, this piece needs energy.

**Haec dies (This Is the Day)** *(William Byrd, 1543-1623)*
This piece by William Byrd, the most respected composer of his generation in England, is a setting in Latin of words from Psalm 118. The same suggestions apply here as for "Sing Joyfully." Keeping a strict pulse makes the cross-rhythms come alive in the "et laetemur" section. The obvious thing is to start the "Alleluias" soft, but in doing so many choirs also slow down. Make a conscious effort not to do this – if nothing else, it will help the basses as they ascend through the clouds!

**The Hunting of the Hare** *(Edward Pearce, c1560-1613?)*
Edward Pearce was organist at St. Paul's Cathedral in London while Thomas Ravenscroft was a treble in the choir. This extraordinary piece can be sung with a rough, rustic tone with the odd shouted "whoope" thrown in. Imagine yourself in a city tavern in early 17th century London near closing time! The "yeeble yabble" bits are very hard, but don't worry if all the notes are not right – it's the spirit of the piece that counts!

**If Ye Love Me** *(Thomas Tallis, c1505-1585)*
Thomas Tallis was, like Thomas Morley and Edward Pearce, a "Gentleman" (i.e. singer!) of the Chapel Royal. In 1575, Queen Elizabeth I granted him, together with William Byrd, exclusive permission to print music, a privilege inherited by Morley in 1598. Tallis is perhaps best known for his simple "Canon" and his far from simple "Spem In Alium," written for 40 voices arranged in eight five-part choirs. The six of us couldn't quite manage "Spem In Alium" when we came to prepare our 1995 RCA album *English Renaissance*, but one of the Tallis numbers we did record on that disc

was this lovely setting of words from St. John's Gospel. The message of the text is very simple. Try and make the way you sing each phrase reflect this: use no vibrato, and don't overdo the phrasing. Again, intonation and blend are all important, as is breath control. Remembering to sing through the phrases will help to achieve a more natural flow of breath.

**A Round of Three Country Dances in One** *(Thomas Ravenscroft, c1582-c1635)*
In each verse the newly-entering voice should sing at full power, while the others accompany, until the final repeat of the last verse, when all voices should sing as loudly as possible. Try to "characterize" this piece as much as possible. It should sound "rough" and "rustic." Imagine a group of farmhands having a sing-song over a few tankards of scrumpy!

**The Silver Swan** *(Orlando Gibbons)*
This is one of the best-known English madrigals, and that is hardly surprising, as it is one of the masterpieces of the English Renaissance. It has been in the King'singers' repertoire for many years, but it is not a piece we take for granted, as it is not as easy as it first appears. Try to avoid making it sound like a soprano tune with accompaniment. Each part is important in its own way. We find that simplicity is the key to a successful performance of this piece, helping Gibbons' sublime music work its magic.

**Sing Joyfully** *(William Byrd)*
A truly joyful setting by William Byrd of words from Psalm 81. This work requires bright, supported singing. Also, it must sound virtuosic, so make sure you don't slow down on the eighth notes.

**The Three Ravens** *(Thomas Ravenscroft)*
The poem in this simple but beautiful piece is a late Medieval allegory on the death of Christ. We find the best approach to this piece is simple and folky: no vibrato, quite free rhythmically and not too earnest or cultured. For instance, the phrase "Down-a-down" sounds good when the "a" is more "er" and is slightly shorter than an eighth note. Also, the word "greene" should be pronounced as two syllables, the final "e" sounding as in "yes." It is good to experiment with various combinations of solo, solo with chorus humming or on "oo" – whatever works best for you.

**Weep, O Mine Eyes** *(John Bennett)*
The text of this simple madrigal is reflected perfectly in the slow, almost painful suspensions in the first two lines. We would use mostly straight tone, no vibrato, except for allowing a little "blossoming" at the height of each individual phrase. Singing the "O when" phrases could be compared to stretching an elastic band until it's about to break! "Intensity" is the key word. Make the most of words like "swell," "high" and "drown." Be careful with intonation – make sure all doubled octaves and fifths (A's and E's) are unanimous and then all other notes should be easier to "place." Try to maintain a slow pulse and above all, make sure you understand what you are singing about. This should communicate the mood of the piece to your audience.

# All Creatures Now Are Merry Minded

For SATBB a cappella

Performance Time: Approx. 1:40

JOHN BENNETT
Edited by THE KING'SINGERS

9
shep - herds' daugh - ters play - ing, the shep - herds' daugh - ters play - ing.
mf
The shep - herds' daugh - ters play - ing, the shep - herds' daugh - ters
shep - herds' daugh - ters play - ing, the shep - herds' daugh - ters play - ing, are
mf
The shep - herds' daugh - ters play - ing, the shep - herds' daugh - ters
shep - herds' daugh - ters play - ing, the shep - herds' daugh - ters play - ing.
9
9
The nymphs are fa - la - la - ing, the nymphs are fa - la - la - ing,
play - ing. The nymphs are fa - la - la - ing, the nymphs are fa - la -
play - ing, are play - ing. The nymphs are fa - la - la - ing, the nymphs are fa - la - la - ing, fa - la - la - la -
play - ing. The nymphs are fa - la - la - ing, the nymphs are fa - la -
The nymphs are fa - la - la - ing, the nymphs are fa - la - la - ing,
13

20
f
the nymphs are fa - la - la - la - la - ing. Yond bu - gle was well
la - ing, the nymphs are fa - la - la - ing. Yond bu - gle was well
la - ing, fa - la - la - la - la - la - la - ing. Yond bu - gle was well
la - ing, the nymphs are fa - la - la - la - la - la - ing. Yond bu - gle was well
the nymphs are fa - la - la - la - la - ing. Yond bu - gle was well
17
wind - ed. At O - ri - a - na's pres - ence each thing smil eth. The
wind - ed. At O - ri - a - na's pres - ence each thing smil - eth. The
wind - ed. At O - ri - a - na's pres - ence each thing smil - eth. The
wind - ed. At O - ri - a - na's pres - ence each thing smil - eth. The
wind - ed. At O - ri - a - na's pres - ence each thing smil - eth. The
21

flow'rs them-selves dis - cov - er, the flow'rs them-selves dis - cov -
flow'rs them-selves dis - cov - er, the flow'rs them-selves dis - cov -
flow'rs them-selves dis - cov - er, the flow'rs them - selves dis - cov -
flow'rs them - selves dis - cov - er, the flow'rs them - selves dis - cov -
flow'rs them - selves _ dis - cov - er, the flow'rs them - selves dis - cov -
26
mp
31
legato
er. Birds o - ver her do hov - er.
er. Birds o - ver her do hov - er.
er. Birds o - ver her do hov - er.
er. Birds o - ver her do hov - er.
er. Birds o - ver her do hov - er.
30

Mu - sic the time be - guil - eth, mu - sic the time be - guil - eth. See
Mu - sic the time be - guil - eth. See
Mu - sic the time be - guil - eth, mu - sic the time be - guil - eth. See
Mu - sic the time be - guil - eth, mu - sic the time be - guil - eth. See
Mu - sic the time be - guil - eth. See
34
39
where she comes, see where she comes, with flow - 'ry gar - lands crown - ed.
where she comes, see where she comes, with flow - 'ry gar - lands crown - ed.
where she comes, see where she comes, with flow - 'ry gar - lands crown - ed.
where she comes, see where she comes, with flow - 'ry gar - lands crown - ed.
where she comes, see where she comes, with flow - 'ry gar - lands crown - ed.
39
39

mf
Queen of all queens re - nown - ed, queen of all
Queen of all queens re - nown - ed, queen of all queens re - nown - ed,
Queen of all queens re - nown - ed, queen of all queens re -
Queen of all queens re - nown - ed, re -
Queen of all queens re - nown - ed, queen of all queens re -
43
49
f
queens re - nown - ed. Then sang the shep - herds and nymphs
re - nown - ed. Then sang the shep - herds and nymphs
nown - ed. Then sang the shep - herds and nymphs
- nown - ed. Then sang the shep - herds and nymphs
nown - ed. Then sang the shep - herds and nymphs
47

56
dim.
of Di - a - na, nymphs of Di - a - na:
dim. mp
of Di - a - na, nymphs of Di - a - na: Long
dim. mp cresc. poco a poco
of Di - a - na, nymphs of Di - a - na: Long live
dim. mp cresc. poco a poco
of Di - a - na, nymphs of Di - a - na: Long
dim. mp cresc. poco a poco
of Di - a - na, nymphs of Di - a - na: Long
dim. mp cresc. poco a poco
52
mp cresc. poco a poco
Long live fair O - ri - a - na,
cresc. poco a poco
live fair O - ri - a - na, long live fair O -
fair O - ri - a - na, long
live fair O - ri - a - na, long
live fair O - ri - a - na, fair
57

O - ri - a - na, fair O - ri - a -
- ri - a - na, O - ri - a - na, long
live, long live fair O - ri - a - na, fair O - ri - a - na,
live fair O - ri - a - na, long live fair O - ri - a -
O - ri - a - na, long live fair O - ri - a -
62
rit.
na, long live fair O - ri - a - na.
live fair O - ri - a - na, fair O - ri - a - na.
fair O - ri - a - na.
- na, fair O - ri - a - na.
- na, fair O - ri - a - na.
67

# As Vesta Was from Latmos Hill Descending

For SSATTB a cappella

Performance Time: Approx. 3:00

THOMAS WEELKES
Edited by THE KING'SINGERS

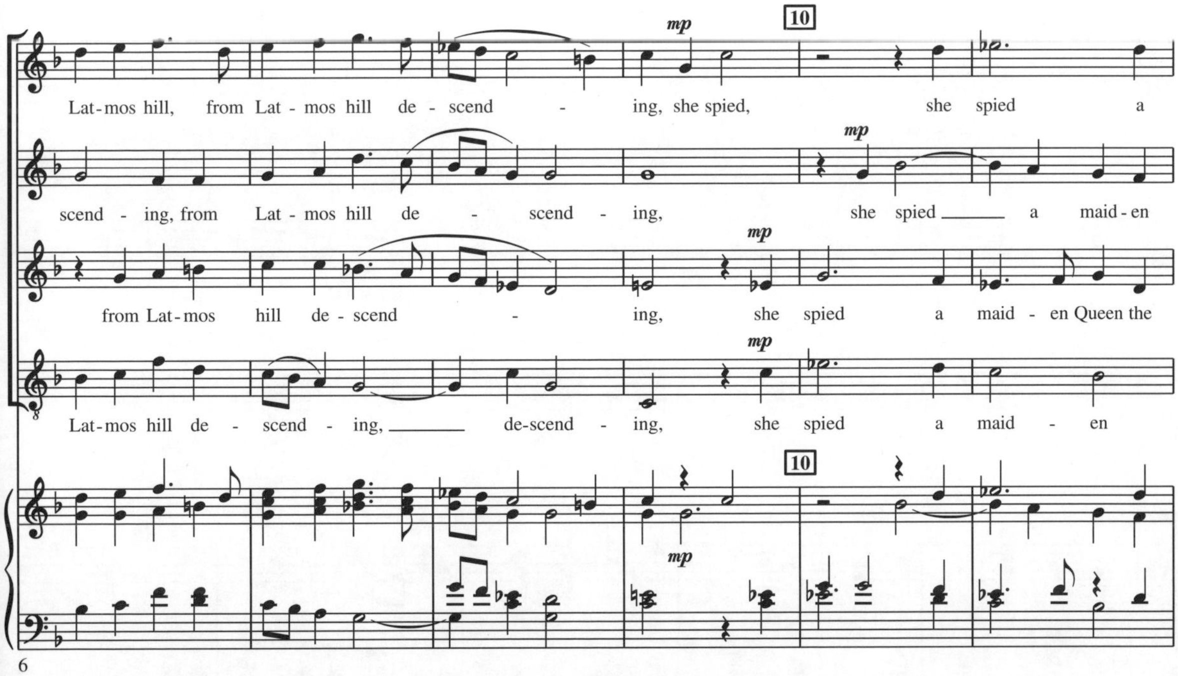

cresc.
maid - en Queen the same a - scend - ing, a - scend -
Queen, she spied a maid - en Queen the same a - scend - ing, a -
same a - scend - ing, a - scend - ing, the same a - scend -
Queen the same a - scend - ing, the same a - scend -
12
- ing, the same a - scend - ing, the same a - scend -
scend - ing, the same a - scend - ing, a - scend -
- ing, a - scend - ing, the same a - scend -
- ing, the same a - scend - ing, the same a - scend -
17

Soprano I
Soprano II
Alto
Tenor I
Tenor II
Bass
23
f
p
22
28
ing, At - tend - ed on by all the shep - herds swain,
ing, At - tend - ed on by all the shep - herds swain,
ing, At - tend - ed on by all the shep - herds swain,
ing, At - tend - ed on by all the shep - herds swain, at -
At - tend - ed on by all the shep - herds swain,
at - tend - ed on by all the shep - herds swain, To
at - tend - ed on by all the shep - herds swain,
at - tend - ed on by all the shep - herds swain, To
tend - ed on by all the shep - herds swain, To
at - tend - ed on by all the shep - herds swain,
At - tend - ed on by all the shep - herds swain, To

33
mf
p
whom Di-a-na's dar - lings, darl - ings came run-ning down a-main, came
To whom Di - a - na's dar - lings came run-ning down a - main, came run-ning down a -
whom Di-a-na's dar - lings, to whom Di - a - na's dar - lings came run-ning
whom Di-a-na's dar - lings came run-ning down a - main, a -
To whom Di - a - na's dar - lings came run-ning down a - main,
whom Di-a-na's dar - lings came run-ning down a-main, came run-ning down a - main,
33
run-ning down a-main, came run-ning down a -
main, came run-ning down a -
down a - main, came run-ning down a - main, came run-ning down a - main,
main, came run-ning down a - main, came
came run-ning down a - main, came run-ning down a - main, a -
came run-ning down a - main, a - main,
38

main, came run-ning down a - main, came run-ning down a - main, came run-ning down a -
main, came run-ning down a - main, came run-ning down a - main, came run-ning down a -
came run-ning down a - main, came run - ning
run-ning down a-main, came run - ning down a - main, came run - ning
main, came run-ning down a-main, a - main, came
came run-ning down a - main, came run - ning
42
48
mp
mf
main, a - main First two by two, then three by three to - geth - er,
main, a - main First two by two, then three by three to - geth - er,
down a - main First two by two, then three by three to - geth - er,
down a - main First two by two, then three by three to - geth - er,
down a - main then three by three to - geth - er,
down a - main then three by three to - geth - er,
46

p
pp
mf
Leav - ing their God - dess all a - lone hast - ed thith - er.
Leav - ing their God - dess hast - ed thith - er. And
Leav - ing their God - dess hast - ed thith - er. And
Leav - ing their God - dess hast - ed thith - er.
Leav - ing their God - dess hast - ed thith - er. And
Leav - ing their God - dess hast - ed thith - er.
53
59
And min - gling with the shep-herds of her train, with
min - gling with the shep-herds of her train, with mirth - ful
min - gling with the shep-herds of her train, of her train, with mirth - ful
And min-gling with the shep-herds of her train, of her
min - gling with the shep-herds of her train, with the shep-herds of her train, with mirth - ful
And min - gling with the shep-herds of her train, with
59

mirth - ful tunes, mirth - ful tunes her pres - ence en - ter - tain,
tunes, with mirth-ful tunes her pres - ence en - ter - tain, her
tunes, with mirth-ful tunes her pres - ence en - ter - tain, her
train, with mirth - ful tunes her pres - ence
tunes, with mirth-ful tunes her pres - ence en - ter - tain, en - ter - tain,
mirth - ful tunes her pres - ence en - ter - tain, her
64
72
f
her pres - ence en - ter - tain. Then sang the shep - herds
pres - ence en - ter - tain. Then sang the shep - herds
pres - ence en - ter - tain. Then sang the shep - herds
en - ter - tain. Then sang the shep -
her pres - ence en - ter - tain. Then sang the shep - herds
pres - ence en - ter - tain. Then sang the shep - herds
69

mp
p
and nymphs of Di - a - na, nymphs of Di - a - na: Long
and nymphs of Di - a - na, nymphs of Di - a - na:
and nymphs of Di - a - na, nymphs of Di - a - na,
herds and nymphs of Di - a - na, nymphs of Di - a - na:
and nymphs of Di - a - na: Long live fair
and nymphs of Di - a - na:
75
80
live fair O - ri - a - na, fair O - ri - a - na, long live fair O - ri - a -
Long live fair O - ri - a - na, O - ri - a - na, long live fair
of Di - a - na: Long live fair O - ri - a - na,
Long live fair O - ri - a - na, long live fair O - ri -
O - ri - a - na, long live fair O - ri - a - na, long
Long live fair O - ri - a - na, long
80
80

na, long live fair O - ri - a - na, long live fair O - ri - a - na,
O - ri - a - na, long live fair O - ri - a - na, long
long live fair O - ri - a - na, long live fair O - ri - a - na, fair
a - na, long live fair O - ri - a - na, fair O - ri -
live fair O - ri - a - na, fair O - ri - a - na, long live fair O - ri -
live
85
cresc. poco a poco
O - ri - a - na, long live fair O - ri - a - na, long live fair O - ri -
live fair O - ri - a - na, long live fair O - ri - a -
O - ri - a - na, long live fair O - ri - a - na, long
a - na, long live fair O - ri - a - na, long live, long live fair O - ri - a -
a - na, long live fair O - ri - a - na, fair O - ri
fair O - ri -
90

a - na, fair O - ri - a - na, long live fair O - ri - a - na, fair
na, long live fair O - ri - a - na, long live fair O - ri - a - na, O - ri - a -
live fair O - ri - a - na, long live fair O - ri -
na, fair O - ri - a - na, long live fair O - ri - a -
a - na, long live fair O - ri - a - na, long live fair
a - na,
95
O - ri - a - na, long live fair O - ri - a - na, fair O - ri - a -
- na, long live fair O - ri - a - na, long live fair O - ri - a -
- a - na, fair O - ri - a - na, long
- na, long live fair O - ri - a - na,
O - ri - a - na, long live fair O - ri - a - na, long live fair
long live fair
100

ff
na, fair O - ri - a - na, long live fair O - ri - a -
ff
na, fair O - ri - a - na, long live fair O - ri - a - na, long
live fair O - ri - a - na, O - ri - a - na,
ff
long live fair O - ri - a - na, long live fair
O - ri - a - na, long live fair O - ri -
ff
O - ri - a - na, long live fair O - ri -
ff
105
rit.
na, long live fair O - ri - a - na.
rit.
live fair O - ri - a - na, long live fair O - ri - a - na.
ff
rit.
long live fair O - ri - a - na, fair O - ri - a - na.
rit.
O - ri - a - na, fair O - ri - a - na.
ff
rit.
a - na, long live fair O - ri - a - na.
rit.
a - na, fair O - ri - a - na.
rit.
110

# Drop, Drop, Slow Tears

For SATB a cappella

Performance Time: Approx. 1:30

**Text by PHINEAS FLETCHER (1582-1650)**

**ORLANDO GIBBONS**
**Edited by THE KING'S SINGERS**

# Fire, Fire

For SATTB a cappella
Performance Time: Approx. 2:20

THOMAS MORLEY
Edited by THE KING'SINGERS

*Original word is "Fyer" (2 syllables)

13
la la la, Fa la la la la la la.
Fire, fire, fire, fire, fire, fire,
O I burn me, O I burn me, O I burn
la la la, Fa la la la la la.
Fire, fire, fire, fire, fire,
O I burn me, O I burn me, O I
la, Fa la la la la la.
Fire, fire, fire, fire,
O I burn me, O I burn
la la la la, Fa la la la la la.
Fire, fire, fire, fire,
O I burn me, O I burn
la la la, Fa la la la la la.
Fire, fire, fire, fire,
O I burn me, O I burn
13
10
fire, fire, my heart, my heart, my heart.
me, O I burn me, a - las, a - las, a - las.
fire, fire, fire, my heart, my heart, my heart.
burn me, O I burn me, a - las, a - las, a - las.
fire, fire, my heart, my heart, my heart.
me, O I burn me, a - las, a - las, a - las.
Fa la la la
fire, fire, my heart, my heart, my heart.
me, O I burn me, a - las, a - las a - las.
Fa la la la la
fire, fire, my heart, my heart, my heart.
me, O I burn me, a - las, a - las, a - las.
Fa la la
15

20
p - f
Fa la la la la la la la la la, Fa la la la la la la.
O
I
Fa la la la la la la la la la, Fa la la la la la.
la, Fa la la la la la la la, Fa la la la la la.
la la la la la, Fa la la la la la la la, Fa la la la la la.
la la la la la la la la la la la la, Fa la la la la la.
20
p - f
20
25
28
p legato
f
help, O help, a - las, O help.
burn, I burn, a - las, I burn.
Ay me, ay
p - f
O help, O help, a - las, O help.
I burn, I burn, a - las, I burn.
Ay me, ay
O help, O help, a - las, O help.
I burn, I burn, a - las, I burn.
Ay me, ay
O help, O help, a - las, O help.
I burn, I burn, a - las, I burn.
Ay me, ay
Ay me, ay
25
28
p legato
f
25

35
me, I sit and cry me
Will none come quench me?
p marcato
me, I sit and cry me and call for
Will none come quench me? O cast, cast
me, I sit and cry me and call for help, a - las, but
Will none come quench me? O cast, cast wa - ter on, a -
me, I sit and cry me and call for help, a - las, but
Will none come quench me? O cast, cast wa - ter on, a -
me, I sit and cry me
Will none come quench me?
31
and call for
O cast, cast
help, a - las, but none comes nigh me, and call for help, a - las,
wa - ter on, a - las, and drench me, O cast, cast wa - ter on,
none comes nigh me, and call for help, a - las,
las, and drench me, O cast, cast wa - ter on,
none comes nigh me, and
las, and drench me, O
and call for help, a - las, but none comes
O cast, cast wa - ter on, a - las, and
36

help, a - las, but none comes nigh me.
wa - ter on, a - las, and drench me.
but none comes nigh me.
a - las, and drench me.
but none comes nigh me, but none comes nigh me. Fa
a - las, and drench me, a - las, and drench me.
very light and lively
call for help, a - las, a - las, but none comes nigh me. Fa la la la
cast, cast wa - ter on, a - las, a - las, and drench me.
very light and lively
nigh me, but none come nigh me. Fa la la la
drench me, a - las, and drench me.
40
44
very light and lively
cresc. poco a poco
Fa la la la la la la, Fa la la la la la la, Fa la
very light and lively
cresc. poco a poco
Fa la la la la la la la, Fa la la la la la la la
very light and lively
cresc. poco a poco
la la la la la la la la, Fa la la, Fa la la la la la la la la la la la, Fa la la la,
cresc. poco a poco
la la la la la, Fa la la la la la la la la la la, Fa la la la
cresc. poco a poco
la la la la la la la, Fa la la la la la la, Fa
44
cresc. poco a poco
44

la la la ___ la la la la la la la ___ la la la la la la la, Fa ___ la la la la
___ la la la la la la la la, Fa la la la, Fa ___ la la la la la, Fa ___ la la
Fa ___ la la la la la la, Fa ___ la la la la la la la,
la la ___ la la la la la, Fa la, Fa la la la la, Fa ___ la la la la, Fa ___
la la la la la la la la, ___ Fa la la la
49
1
(D.C.)
2
f
ff
rit.
la la la, Fa la la la la. la la la, Fa la la la.
la la la la, Fa la la la. la la la la, Fa la la la la la la la la la la la.
Fa la la la la la la. Fa la la la la la la la la la la la.
___ la la la la la la la. ___ la la la la la, Fa la la la la la.
la, Fa la la la. la, Fa la la la.
54

# Haec dies
## (This Is the Day)

For SSATTB a cappella
Performance Time: Approx. 2:00

**Latin Text: Psalm 118:24**
**English Text by PHILIP LAWSON**

**WILLIAM BYRD**
**Edited by THE KING'SINGERS**

Haec di - es quam fe - cit Do -
This is the day, the day the Lord
nus. Haec di - es
made. This is the day,
Do - mi - nus, quam fe - cit Do - mi-nus.
the day, the day the Lord has made.
f
Haec di - es quam fe - cit Do - mi - nus, Do -
This is the day which the Lord, the Lord has made, the Lord
nus, quam fe - cit Do - mi - nus.
made, the day the Lord, the Lord has made.
di - es quam fe - cit Do - mi-nus, quam fe - cit
is the day which the Lord has made, has made, the day the
9
- mi - nus, quam fe - cit Do - mi -
has made, the day the Lord has
quam fe - cit Do - mi - nus, quam
the day the Lord has made, the
Haec di - es quam
This is the day, the
- mi - nus. Haec di - es quam fe - cit Do - mi-nus,
has made. This is the day which the Lord, the Lord has made,
Haec di - es quam fe - cit Do - mi-nus,
This is the day, the day the Lord has made,
Do - mi-nus. Haec di - es quam fe - cit
Lord has made. This is the day which the Lord has
13

nus, quam fe - cit Do - mi - nus, quam fe - cit Do -
made, the day the Lord has made, the day the Lord
fe - cit Do - mi - nus, quam fe - cit Do - mi - nus, Do -
day the Lord has made, the day the Lord has made, the
fe - cit Do - mi - nus, quam fe - cit
day the Lord has made, the day the
quam fe - cit Do - mi - nus, quam fe - cit Do -
the day the Lord has made, the day the Lord
quam fe - cit Do - mi - nus, quam fe - cit Do - mi - nus,
the day the Lord has made, the day the Lord has made,
Do - mi - nus, quam fe - cit Do - mi - nus, quam fe - cit
made, has made, the day the Lord has made, the day the
17
(♩ = ♩)
23
- mi - nus. Ex - ul - te - mus, ex - ul -
has made. Let us praise him, let us
- mi - nus. Ex - ul - te - mus
Lord has made. Let us praise him;
Do - mi - nus. Ex - ul - te - mus
Lord has made. Let us praise him;
- mi - nus. Ex - ul -
has made. Let us
Do - mi - nus. Ex - ul - te - mus, ex - ul -
Lord has made. Let us praise him, let us
Do - mi - nus. Ex - ul -
Lord has made. Let us
(♩ = ♩)
23
21

te - mus et lae - te - mur in e -
praise him; sing with glad - ness and with
et lae - te - mur
sing with glad - ness
et lae - te - mur, et lae - te - mur, et lae - te - mur
sing with glad - ness, sing with glad - ness, sing with glad - ness
te - mus et lae - te - mur, et lae - te - mur, et lae - te - mur
praise him; sing with glad - ness, sing with glad - ness, sing with glad - ness
te - mus et lae - te - mur, et lae - te - mur
praise him; sing with glad - ness, sing with glad - ness
te - mus et lae - te - mur
praise him; sing with glad - ness
26
32
- a. Ex - ul - te - mus,
joy. Let us praise him,
Ex - ul - te - mus
Let us praise him;
in e - a. Ex - ul - te - mus, ex - ul - te -
and with joy. Let us praise him, let us praise
in e - a. Ex - ul -
and with joy. Let us
in e - a. Ex - ul - te - mus, ex - ul - te - mus
and with joy. Let us praise him, let us praise him;
Ex - ul - te - mus,
Let us praise him,
30

ex - ul - te - mus et lae - te - mur
let us praise him; sing with glad - ness
et lae - te - mur,
sing with glad - ness,
- mus, ex - ul - te - mus et lae - te - mur, et lae - te - mur,
him, let us praise him; sing with glad - ness, sing with glad - ness,
te - mus et lae - te - mur, et lae - te - mur,
praise him; sing with glad - ness, sing with glad - ness,
et lae - te - mur, et lae - te - mur, et lae - te - mur,
sing with glad - ness, sing with glad - ness, sing with glad - ness,
ex - ul - te - mus et lae - te - mur,
let us praise him; sing with glad - ness,
34
in e - a, et lae - te - mur in e - a.
and with joy, sing with glad - ness and with joy.
et lae - te - mur, et lae - te - mur in e -
sing with glad - ness, sing with glad - ness and with
et lae - te - mur in e - a, in e -
sing with glad - ness and with joy, and with
et lae - te - mur in e - a, in e -
sing with glad - ness and with joy, and with
et lae - te - mur, et lae - te - mur in e - a, in e -
sing with glad - ness, sing with glad - ness and with joy, and with
et lae - te - mur in e -
sing with glad - ness and with
38

43
(♩ = ♩)
p cresc. poco a poco
Al - le - lu - ia. Al - le - lu -
a.
joy.
Al - le - lu - ia.
Al - le - lu - ia.
Al - le - lu -
Al - le - lu - ia.
cresc. poco a poco
42
ia.
Al - le - lu - ia. Al - le - lu -
Al - le - lu -
ia.
Al - le - lu - ia. Al - le - lu -
Al - le - lu - ia.
47

Al - le - lu - ia. Al - le - lu -
ia. Al - le - lu -
ia. Al - le - lu -
Al - le - lu - ia.
ia. Al - le - lu -
Al - le - lu - ia.
52
ia. Al -
ia. Al - le - lu - ia.
- ia. Al - le - lu -
Al - le - lu - ia.
- ia. Al - le - lu -
Al - le - lu - ia.
57

- le - lu - ia. Al - le - lu - ia. Al - le-lu - ia.
Al - le - lu -
ia. Al - le - lu - ia. Al - le-lu - ia. Al - le -
Al - le - lu - ia. Al-le - lu - ia. Al-
ia. Al-le - lu-ia. Al - le - lu -
Al - le - lu - ia.
62
Al - le - lu - ia. Al - le-lu -
ia. Al - le - lu -
lu - ia.
- le - lu - ia. Al - le -
ia. Al - le - lu - ia.
Al - le - lu - ia.
67

ff
ia. Al - le - lu - ia. Al - le - lu - ia.
- ia. Al - le - lu -
Al - le - lu - ia. Al - le -
lu - ia. Al - le - lu - ia.
Al - le - lu - ia.
Al - le - lu - ia. Al - le -
71
rit.
Al - le - lu - ia. Al - le - lu - ia.
ia. Al - le - lu - ia. Al - le - lu - ia.
lu - ia. Al - le - lu - ia.
Al - le - lu - ia.
Al - le - lu - ia. Al - le - lu - ia.
lu - ia. Al - le - lu - ia.
76

# The Hunting of the Hare

For TTBB a cappella

Performance Time: Approx. 1:25

EDWARD PEARCE
Edited by THE KING'SINGERS
from an Edition Prepared by
JOHN DOUGLAS WILLIAMS

hoick, hoick - a hoick, whoope, whoope, whoope, whoope,
- a hoick, hoick - a hoick, whoope, whoope, whoope, whoope, whoope,
there, hoick - a hoick, whoope, whoope, whoope, whoope, whoope,
hoick - a hoick, hoick - a hoick, whoope, whoope, whoope, whoope,
11
16
crie, there they goe, crie, there they goe, they goe, they goe, they
crie, there they goe, crie, there they goe, they goe, they goe, they
crie, there they goe, crie, there they goe, they goe, they goe, they
crie, there they goe, crie, there they goe, they goe, they goe, they
16
16

*Re-articulate the "h" on each eighth note.

* Pronounced *tee-oo*

39
full crie, With yee-ble yab-ble gib-ble gab-ble hey, with yee-ble yab-ble gib-ble gab-ble
full crie, With yee-ble yab-ble gib-ble gab-ble hey, with yee-ble yab-ble
full crie, With yee-ble yab-ble gib-ble gab-ble hey, with
full crie, With yee-ble yab-ble gib-ble gab-ble hey, with
39
38
hey, with gib - ble gab - ble hey, with yee - ble yab - ble gib - ble gab - ble
gib - ble gab - ble hey, with hey, with yee - ble yab - ble gib - ble gab - ble
yee - ble yab - ble, yee - ble yab - ble gib - ble gab - ble hey, with yee - ble yab - ble gib - ble gab - ble
yee - ble yab - ble gib - ble gab - ble hey, with yee - ble yab - ble gib - ble gab - ble
42

47
hey, with hey. The hounds doe knocke it lust - i -
yee - ble yab - ble gib - ble gab - ble hey. The hounds doe knocke it lust - i -
yee - ble yab - ble gib - ble gab - ble hey. The hounds doe knocke it lust - i -
yee - ble yab - ble gib - ble gab - ble hey. The hounds doe knocke it lust - i -
47
45

rit. (2nd time)
1
2
ly, with o - pen mouth and _ lus - tie crie. With crie.
rit. (2nd time)
ly, with o - pen mouth and _ lus - tie crie. crie.
rit. (2nd time)
ly, with o - pen mouth and lus - tie crie. With crie.
rit. (2nd time)
ly, with o - pen mouth and lus - tie crie. crie.
1
2
rit. (2nd time)
49

# If Ye Love Me

For SATB a cappella

Performance Time: Approx. 2:35

**Text: John 14:15-17a**

**THOMAS TALLIS**
**Edited by THE KING'SINGERS**

10
give you an - oth - er com - fort - er,
he shall give you an - oth - er com - fort - er,
he shall give you an - oth - er com - fort - er, that
and he shall give you an - oth - er com - fort - er,
10
10
14
mp - p
that he may bide with you for ev -
mp - p
that he may bide with you for ev - er, with you for ev -
(mp - p)
he may bide with you for ev - er, that he may bide with you for ev -
mp - p
that he may bide with you for ev - er, may bide with you for ev -
14
(mp - p)
14

20
er, ev'n the spirit of truth,
er, ev'n the spirit of truth, ev'n the spirit of
er, ev'n the spirit of truth, the spirit of truth, ev'n
er, ev'n the spirit of truth, the spirit of truth,
20
19
1
2
ev'n the spirit of truth, ev'n the spirit of truth, truth.
truth, ev'n the spirit of truth, ev'n the spirit of truth, truth.
p
the spirit of truth, the spirit of truth, the spirit of truth, that truth.
ev'n the spirit of truth, the spirit of truth, truth.
1
2
23

# A Round of Three Country Dances in One

For TTBB a cappella

Performance Time: Approx. 1:50

**THOMAS RAVENSCROFT**
**Edited by THE KING'SINGERS**

*See Performance Notes for suggested dynamics.

25
dance be - fore the Queen - a. In a red
toy that sel - dom is seen - a. Sing coun - try
(Three)
21
pet - ti - coat and a green jack - et, a white hose and a
danc - es in one to be, a pret - ty con - ceit as
26
Tenor I
33
2nd time
Now foot it as I do Tom boy Tom, now
Bass I
green - a. Rob - in Hood, Rob - in Hood, said lit - tle John, come
Bass II
I ween - a. Three af - ter fel - lows as you hear me, a
(Sing)
33
31

41
foot it as I do Swith - en - a. Now Hick thou must trick it
(And)
dance be - fore the Queen - a. In a red pet - ti - coat
toy that sel - dom is seen - a. Sing coun - try danc - es in
(Three)
41
37
all a - lone, till Rob - in come leap - ing in be - tween -
and a green jack - et, a white hose and a green -
one to be, a pret - ty con - ceit as I ween -
43
Tenor I
49
a. And foot it as I do Tom boy Tom, now
(Now)
Tenor II
2nd time
The cramp is in my purse full sore, no
Bass I
a. Rob - in Hood, Rob - in Hood, said lit - tle John, come
Bass II
a. Three af - ter fel - lows as you hear me, a
(Sing)
49
48

57
foot it as I do Swith - en - a. Now foot it as
mon - ey will bide there - in - a. The cramp is
dance be - fore the Queen - a. Rob - in Hood,
toy that sel - dom is seen - a. Sing af - ter
57
53
I do Tom boy Tom, now foot it as I do
in my purse full sore, no mon - ey will bide there -
Rob - in Hood, said lit - tle John, come dance be - fore the
fel - lows as you hear me, a toy that sel - dom
58

65
Swith - en - a. And Hick thou must trick it all a -
in - a.
Queen - a. In a red pet - ti - coat and a green
is seen - a. Three coun - try danc - es in one to
65
63
lone, till Rob - in come leap - ing in be - tween -
Hey ho, the cramp - a.
jack - et, a white hose and a green -
be, a pret - ty con - ceit as I ween -
68

73
a. And Hick thou must trick it all a - lone, till
Hey ho, the cramp - a. Hey
a. In a red pet - ti - coat and a green jack - et, a
a. Three coun - try danc - es in one to be, a
73
72
rit. (2nd time)
1
2
Rob - in come leap - ing in be - tween - a. Now a.
ho, the cramp - a, the cramp - a. The a.
white hose and a green - a. a.
pret - ty con - ceit as I ween - a. Sing a.
77

# The Silver Swan

For SATBB a cappella
Performance Time: Approx. 1:20

ORLANDO GIBBONS
Edited by THE KING'SINGERS

7
mp
throat; Lean - ing her breast a -
throat; Lean - ing her breast a - gainst the reed - y
throat; Lean - ing her breast a - gainst the
throat; a - gainst the reed - y shore,
throat; Lean - ing her breast a - gainst the reed - y
7
gainst the reed - y shore, thus sung her first and last, and sung no
shore, thus sung her first and last, and sung no more, no
reed - y shore, thus sung her first and last, and sung no
thus sung her first and last, and sung no more, and sung no
shore, thus sung her first and last, and sing no
mf
10

14
pp
more. Fare - well, all joys, O death come close mine
more. Fare - well, all joys, O death come close mine eyes; More
more. Fare - well, all joys, O death come close mine eyes;
more. Fare - well, all joys, O death come close mine
more. Fare - well, all joys, O death come close mine eyes;
14
pp
14
poco rit.
eyes; More geese than swans now live, more fools than wise.
geese than swans now live, more fools than wise, than wise.
More geese than swans now live, more fools than wise.
eyes; More geese than swans now live, more fools than wise.
More geese than swans now live, more fools than wise.
18

# Sing Joyfully

For SSATTB a cappella

Performance Time: Approx. 2:10

**Text: Psalm 81:1-4**

**WILLIAM BYRD**
**Edited by THE KING'SINGERS**

10
strength. Sing loud, sing loud un - to the God of
our strength. Sing loud, sing loud,
our strength. Sing loud, sing loud un - to the
Sing loud un - to the God of Ja - cob,
our strength. Sing loud, sing loud un - to the God of
Sing loud, sing loud un - to the
10
9
Ja - cob, un - to the God of Ja - cob.
sing loud un - to the God of Ja - cob.
God of Ja - cob, un - to the God of Ja - cob. Take the
un - to the God of Ja - cob. Take
Ja - cob, the God of Ja - cob. Take
God of Ja - cob, un - to the God of Ja - cob.
13

17
p
Take the song, and bring forth the tim - brel, and bring forth the
p
Take the song, and bring forth the tim - brel, and bring forth the
song, take the song, song, the song, and bring forth the tim -
the song, the song, the song, the song, and bring forth the tim - brel,
the song, the song, the song, and bring forth the tim - brel, and bring forth the
p
Take the song, song, take the song, and bring forth the
17
17
cresc.
tim - brel, the pleas-ant harp, the pleas-ant harp and the vi -
tim - brel, the pleas-ant harp and the vi - ol,
- brel, the pleas-ant harp and the vi - ol, the pleas - ant harp,
cresc.
the tim - brel, the pleas-ant harp and the vi - ol,
cresc.
tim - brel, the pleas-ant harp and the vi - ol, the pleas - ant
cresc.
tim - brel, the pleas - ant harp, the pleas-ant harp and the vi - ol, and the
cresc.
21

26
ol, and the vi - ol. Blow the trum-pet in the new moon, in ___ the new
the pleas-ant harp and the vi - ol, and the vi - ol. Blow the trum - pet
the pleas-ant harp and the vi - ol. Blow the trum-pet in the new moon, blow the
the vi - ol, and ___ the ___ vi - ol. Blow the trum - pet
harp, pleas - ant harp and the vi - ol. Blow the trum-pet in the new moon, blow the
vi - ol, and the vi - ol. Blow the trum-pet in the new moon, blow the
24
moon, in ___ the new moon, blow the trum - pet in the new
in the new moon, in ___ the new moon, in the new moon, blow the
trum - pet in the new moon, in ___ the new moon, blow the trum - pet, blow the
in the new moon, blow the trum - pet in ___ the new moon, ___ in the new
trum - pet in the new moon, in the new moon, ___ blow the
trum - pet in the new moon, blow the trum - pet in the new
dim.
28

mp
35
moon, in the new moon. Ev'n in the time ap - point -
trum - pet in the new moon, in the new moon.
mp
trum - pet, blow the trum - pet in the new moon. Ev'n in the time ap - point -
mp
moon, in the new moon. Ev'n in the
mp
trum - pet in the new moon, in the new moon. Ev'n in the time ap -
mp
moon, blow the trum - pet in the new moon. Ev'n in the time ap -
35
dim.
mp
32
f
ed, ap - point - ed, ev'n in the time ap - point - ed, and at our
mp
f
Ev'n in the time ap - point - ed, and
f
ed, ev'n in the time ap - point - ed, and at our
time ap - point - ed, ev'n in the time ap - point - ed,
f
point - ed, ev'n in the time ap - point - ed, and
point - ed, ev'n in the time ap - point -
f
36

feast day, and at our feast day, and at our feast day.
mf
at our feast day, our feast day, and at our feast, our feast day. For
mf
feast day, and at our feast day, and at our feast day. For
f
mf
and at our feast day, our feast day, and at our feast day. For
mf
at our feast day, and at our feast day, our feast day. For
f
mf
ed, and at our feast day, and at our feast day. For
mf
40
44
mf
For this is a statute for Is - ra - el,
mp
this is a stat - ute for Is - ra - el, and a
mp
this is a stat - ute for Is - ra - el, and a law
this is a stat - ute for Is - ra - el,
this, for this is a stat - ute for Is - ra - el,
mp
this is a stat - ute for Is - ra - el, and a
44
mp
44

48
mp cresc. poco a poco
of the God of Ja - cob,
cresc. poco a poco
law of the God of Ja - cob, of Ja - cob,
cresc. poco a poco
of the God of Ja - cob, and a law of the
mp cresc. poco a poco
and a law of the God
mp cresc. poco a poco
and a law of the God of Ja - cob,
cresc. poco a poco
law of the God of Ja - cob, of Ja - cob, and a law of the
48
cresc. poco a poco
48

and a law of the God of Ja - cob,
of the God of Ja - cob,
God of Ja - cob, of the God of Ja - cob,
of Ja - cob, and a law of the
and a law of the God of Ja - cob, of the God
God of Ja - cob, of Ja - cob, of the God of
52

of the God of Ja - cob, and a
and a law of the God of Ja - cob, and a
and a law of the God of Ja - cob, of Ja - cob,
God of Ja - cob, and a law of the God of Ja -
of Ja - cob, Ja - cob, and a law of the God of Ja -
Ja - cob, of the God of Ja - cob, and a law
56
law of the God of Ja - cob.
law of the God of Ja - cob.
and a law of the God of Ja - cob.
cob, of the God of Ja - cob.
cob, of the God of Ja - cob.
of the God of Ja - cob.
rit.
60

# The Three Ravens

For SATB a cappella

Performance Time: Approx. 3:00

**THOMAS RAVENSCROFT**
**Edited by J.S. JACKMAN**

8
on a tree, With a down, There were three Rav'ns sat
green - e field, For down in yon - der
on a tree, With a down, There were three Rav'ns sat
green - e field, For down in yon - der
on a tree, With a down, There were three Rav'ns sat
green - e field, For down in yon - der
on a tree, With a down, There were three Rav'ns sat
green - e field, For down in yon - der
8
6
on a tree, They were as black as
green - e field, A knight lies slain be -
on a tree, They were as black as
green - e field, A knight lies slain be -
on a tree, They were as black as
green - e field, A knight lies slain be -
on a tree, They were as black as
green - e field, A knight lies slain be -
9

3. Now down there comes a fallow doe,
   Down-a-down, hey down-a-down,
   Now down there comes a fallow doe,
   With a down,
   Now down there comes a fallow doe,
   As great with child as she might go,
   With a down, derry, derry, derry down, down.

4. She lifted up his bloody head,
   Down-a-down, hey down-a-down,
   She lifted up his bloody head,
   With a down,
   She lifted up his bloody head,
   And kiss'd his wounds that were so red,
   With a down, derry, derry, derry down, down.

5. She buried him before the prime,
   Down-a-down, hey down-a-down,
   She buried him before the prime,
   With a down,
   She buried him before the prime,
   Was dead herself ere ev'nsong time,
   With a down, derry, derry, derry down, down.

# Weep, O Mine Eyes

For SATB a cappella

Performance Time: Approx. 2:40

JOHN BENNETT
Edited by THE KING'SINGERS

eyes, and cease not. A -
O mine eyes, and cease not. A - las, these,
O mine eyes, and cease not. A - las,
weep and cease not, and cease not.
11
las, these, your spring tides, a - las,
your spring tides, a - las, these, your spring
these, your spring tides, a - las,
A - las, these, your spring tides,
17

these, your spring tides, me thinks in - crease
tides, me thinks in - crease not, me thinks in - crease
these, your spring tides, me thinks in - crease
in - crease not, me thinks in - crease
23
29
mp - pp
not. O when, O when
not. O when, O when
not. O when, O when be -
not. O when, O when be -
29
mp - pp
28

be - gin you to swell so high that I may drown me in
be - gin you to swell so high that I may drown me in
gin you to swell so high that I may drown, that I may drown me in
gin you to swell so high that I may drown me in
34
1
2
you, that I may drown me in you? you?
you, that I may drown me in you? you?
you, that I may drown me in you? you?
you, that I may drown me in you? you?
1
2
39